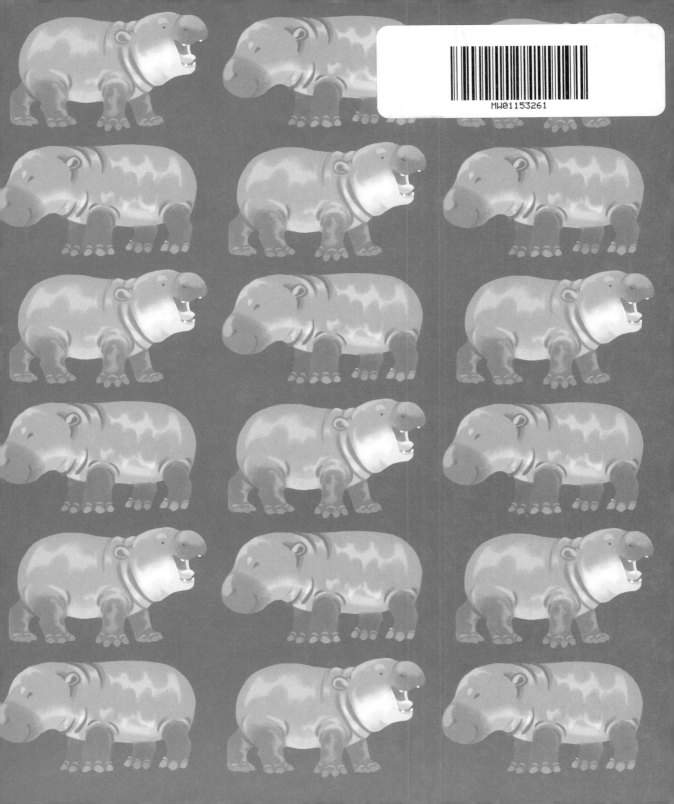

MW01153261

YOUNG ZOOLOGIST
PYGMY HIPPO

A FIRST FIELD GUIDE TO
MOO DENG AND FRIENDS

NEON SQUID

CONTENTS

3

HELLO YOUNG ZOOLOGIST!

Welcome to the world of pygmy hippos! My name is Fiona, and I am a scientist from Leicestershire, England. I work at the Zoological Society of London, and I have been studying and working with large herbivores for many years. I cannot wait to share everything I have learned with you. Do you want to know more about these amazing water-loving animals? Then let's explore their world together!

DR. FIONA SACH

FACT FILE

SCIENTIFIC NAME
Choeropsis liberiensis

CLASS
Mammal

FAMILY
Hippopotamidae

HABITAT
Tropical rainforests and swampy areas around rivers and streams

LIFESPAN
25–30 years in the wild and 30–50 years in zoos

WEIGHT
400–600 lb (180–275 kg)

CONSERVATION STATUS
Endangered with a decreasing population

WHERE THEY LIVE
The largest population is in Liberia, West Africa. Smaller populations can be found in Sierra Leone, Guinea, and Côte d'Ivoire. The pygmy hippo's range does not overlap with the common hippo's.

SIZE COMPARISON

Pygmy hippo:
30–40 in
(75–100 cm) tall

Common hippo:
4–5 ft (1.2–1.5 m) tall

BEFORE YOU GET STARTED

1 RAIN BOOTS
Pygmy hippos live near water, so the right boots can help you walk across wet and muddy ground. Rain boots can also protect your legs from plants and roots.

2 BUG SPRAY
Heat and water equals insects—including mosquitos. These critters can carry diseases, so it is important to wear insect repellent.

3 SUNSCREEN AND HAT
Pygmy hippos live in wet and sunny places. A wide-brimmed hat will help to keep you cool and dry, while sunscreen is essential to protect your skin from sunburn.

4 NOTEBOOK AND PEN
All scientists need to collect information in the field. You can use a notebook and pen to write down all your observations. Because the forest can be wet and damp, bring a plastic bag to keep your notebook dry!

Pygmy hippos live in densely forested areas that can be hot and humid. They like to spend time on land and in water, so you'll need to be prepared for both situations. Here are some things you'll need to pack when setting off in search of these shy creatures.

5 SAMPLE CONTAINERS
To study pygmy hippos you will need to collect samples in containers. You can collect samples of the plants they eat, the water that they swim in, the soil in areas where they live, and samples of their poop! You can take these back to the lab for further study.

6 FANNY PACK
In the field, a fanny pack can be super handy. You can use it to hold things you need to grab fast, like a tape measure to check sizes and distances. You can store bug spray and sunscreen in your fanny pack, too.

7 CAMERA TRAPS
Pygmy hippos are very elusive and most active at night, so scientists use special cameras to see what they are doing and how they are using their environment. Camera traps are left in the wild to take pictures or videos of animals when humans are not around.

MEET THE PYGMY HIPPO

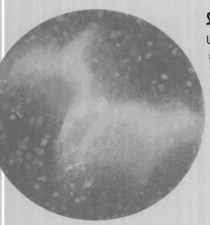

SHINY SKIN

Unlike common hippos, pygmy hippos release an oily substance from their skin called blood sweat. This helps make them waterproof, protects them against infections, and acts like a natural sunscreen!

WEBBED TOES

Pygmy hippos have four toes on each foot. The toes have webbing between them, like a frog's, and make them better swimmers. The pygmy hippo's webbed feet also make it easier for them to walk on the muddy ground around the swamps where they live.

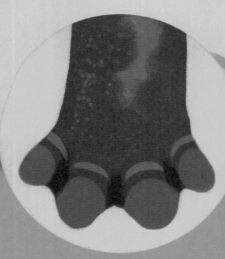

FUNNY TUMMY

Most mammals have just one stomach chamber to break down their varied diets. But pygmy hippos have several stomach chambers to digest all the plants they eat. Bacteria living inside their gut helps with this.

Pygmy hippos might just look like a small version of the common hippo, but they are actually a different species. From its tummy to its toes, a pygmy hippo's body is fascinating. Let's take a closer look.

OPEN WIDE

At first glance, it may not look like pygmy hippos have many teeth. But in fact, they have 34 teeth that grow throughout their lives. They use them to grind up their food. Occasionally, they also use them to scare away rivals!

STUBBY LEGS

Pygmy hippos have short legs. Their smaller size allows them to move through the forest's undergrowth more easily than larger animals.

THE FAMILY

COMMON HIPPO

Common hippos are up to six times heavier than pygmy hippos! They can be found in rivers and lakes during the day and feeding on open grasslands at night. Unlike pygmy hippos, the common hippo is incredibly social. They live together in groups of up to 30 individuals.

WHALES

A whale's blood and muscles store oxygen so that they can spend long periods of time underwater without needing to come up for air.

Pygmy hippos are in the same family as the much larger common hippo. You might be surprised to learn that the hippo family's closest living relatives are whales and dolphins, who adapted over time to be able to live in water.

ANTHRACOTHERES

Around 2.5 million years ago, these mammals could be seen wandering Europe, Africa, North America, and Asia. They looked like a cross between a hippo and a pig. Some species of anthracotheres were even smaller than pygmy hippos! Climate change and competition from other animals caused them to go extinct.

DOLPHINS

Dolphins are some of the most intelligent animals on Earth. When they sleep, bottlenose dolphins switch off one half of their brain. This allows them to rest but also keep an eye out for danger.

HOME SWEET HOME

KEEPING IT COOL

Pygmy hippos have delicate skin. The thick trees in rainforests provide them with shade and protection from the sun's heat as well as plenty of vegetation to chomp on.

SPLASHING AROUND

Pygmy hippos always live near water. They love wallowing in mud during the day to keep cool and prevent their skin from drying out.

Animals choose their habitats based on the things they need to survive. The pygmy hippo's habitat provides them with food to eat, water to drink and cool off in, and safe places to rest. It's a pygmy hippo paradise!

SMILE!

These cameras take photos or videos every time they detect movement in front of them. Scientists then study these images to monitor pygmy hippo populations and behavior. More recently, devices have been placed by scientists in the forests to record the sounds that pygmy hippos make.

DINNER IS SERVED

PLANTS, PLEASE!

Pygmy hippos eat lots of different types of forest plants, including roots, grasses, herbs, the stems and leaves of young trees, and aquatic plants. They also eat fallen fruit, and they have even been known to eat human crops!

LOW AND SLOW

Pygmy hippos have a slow metabolism, which means that it takes their bodies a long time to turn the food they eat into energy. The plants they eat are low in calories and provide just the right amount of energy to meet the pygmy hippo's daily needs.

Pygmy hippos love to eat! They can spend up to six hours a day eating, mostly from midday into the night. Hooray for midnight feasts! They usually only eat plants, with one very curious exception…

FERN-TASTIC

Pygmy hippos especially like ferns. They have been seen standing on their back legs and reaching up to nibble on ferns growing high up in palm trees!

GONE FISHING

Pygmy hippos have been seen eating fish from traps in Sierra Leone. This is very unusual behavior!

CHANGING THE ECOSYSTEM

MIXING IT UP

As pygmy hippos move through water, they stir up the depths. This helps to refresh the habitat for amphibians, fish, and plants by providing fresh food sources.

BLAZING A TRAIL

Pygmy hippos create trails while moving through the forest. Other animals use these trails to move between feeding grounds and water more easily.

POOP ALERT!

When pygmy hippos poop, they whip their tails from side to side. This spreads nutrients and seeds they've eaten back into the soil so new plants can grow.

Despite their small size, pygmy hippos have a huge impact on their ecosystem. They can change how an area looks and what seeds grow where. Never underestimate a pygmy hippo—they play an important role in regenerating the forest!

KEEPING THINGS TIDY

Pygmy hippos graze on lots of leaves and grasses. This helps stop areas of the forest from becoming overgrown.

LIFE CYCLE

1 MOM AND DAD

Pygmy hippos love water, and it's believed that they mate both in water and on land. They can reproduce throughout the year.

2 BUNS IN THE OVEN

A female pygmy hippo—called a cow— is pregnant for around 188 days before giving birth. She usually gives birth on land to a single calf. Only around 1 in 200 births are twins—it's very rare!

Pygmy hippos spend most of their lives alone. Adult males and females come together to breed before going their separate ways again. So how does a female pygmy hippo care for her young? And how do calves learn to look after themselves?

3 HAPPY BIRTHDAY!
Pygmy hippo calves weigh around 10–13 lb (4.5–6 kg) when they're born. They do not follow their mothers around. Instead, she "parks" them somewhere safe and secluded and returns at regular intervals to feed them.

4 GOING IT ALONE
Pygmy hippos stay with their mothers for up to two years to learn essential survival skills. Gradually, they begin to become more independent and start to venture off on their own.

THREATS

DEFORESTATION

The forests where pygmy hippos live are being chopped down to make space for farming, mining, and housing. This means that pygmy hippos have fewer places to live, and their habitat becomes fragmented, making it difficult for them to find suitable mates.

Pygmy hippos are endangered and there are only around 2,500 left in the wild. Human behavior and climate change are both to blame. Some local communities are trying to help protect pygmy hippos to stop their numbers falling even further.

HUNTING

Pygmy hippos are hunted for their meat and for specific body parts—such as their skulls—which are used in traditional medicine. Anti-poaching groups have been set up in some places to guard the forests and help protect pygmy hippos.

CLIMATE CHANGE

Changes in rainfall affect the muddy swamps where pygmy hippos like to wallow. If there is less rain, the swamps dry out and pygmy hippos cannot use them.

HOW YOU CAN HELP

HIPPOS IN HUMAN CARE

Zoos play an important role in supporting pygmy hippo conservation by breeding these endangered animals to increase their population. Zoos also carry out scientific research that can help pygmy hippos in the wild.

SAVE OUR PLANET!!

MAKE YOUR VOICE HEARD

You could donate to, raise money for, or volunteer with organizations that are working to protect pygmy hippos and the precious forests in West Africa where they live. You can also organize or join a march to bring attention to the threats to pygmy hippos and their environment.

We can all do our bit for pygmy hippos. Visiting zoos to learn more about conservation efforts, getting the word out about the pygmy hippo's plight, and buying eco-friendly products are all ways you can help this amazing species survive. All is not lost!

DO YOUR BIT

Look out for the Forest Stewardship Council logo on packaging and products. Whenever you see this logo, it means that the item has been made with trees from a sustainable forest where the animals and people living in and around the forest have been considered.

MOO DENG

MOO DENG

Moo Deng lives at the Khao Kheow Open Zoo in Thailand with her siblings and mom. Her name was chosen by the public and translates to "bouncy pork."

MAKING FRIENDS?

Moo Deng sometimes playfully tries to bite her zookeeper. Despite its small size, an adult pygmy hippo has a bite force stronger than a grizzly bear's!

THE RACE IS ON

Moo Deng enjoys nothing more than a quick dash around her enclosure. Pygmy hippos can reach speeds of up to 19 mph (30 kph). Despite being much bigger, common hippos can run at 30 mph (48 kph)!

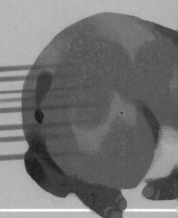

In September 2024, two-month-old Moo Deng appeared on social media in a post from her zoo in Thailand. Since then, the world has become obsessed with this sassy pygmy hippo. But how much is Moo Deng like her wild cousins?

TIME FOR A BATH

In the wild, pygmy hippos love to spend their time bathing in swamps. However, it seems that Moo Deng isn't as big a fan of bath time as her relatives. She runs away from her zookeeper when they try to hose her down!

HUNGRY HIPPOS

Moo Deng can often be seen with grass or vegetables hanging from her mouth, even though she's still too young to eat solid food. Like wild pygmy hippos, Moo Deng is copying her mom to learn important survival skills.

SWEET DREAMS

Pygmy hippos spend over half their time sleeping, and Moo Deng is no exception. Pygmy hippos can hold their breath for up to 15 minutes, allowing them to sleep underwater.

MYTHOLOGY

SHINE BRIGHT

One folktale says that the pygmy hippo finds its way through the dark forest at night by carrying a diamond in its mouth. The diamond helps to light the pygmy hippo's path. By day, the hippo is said to hide the diamond away where it cannot be found. Other tales tell of the pygmy hippo warning humans not to harm the forest or they will face severe consequences...

Deep in the dense forest where pygmy hippos live, all sorts of weird and wonderful creatures exist. Pygmy hippos are rarely seen by local people, making them even more mysterious and magical. Because of this, they feature in many folktales.

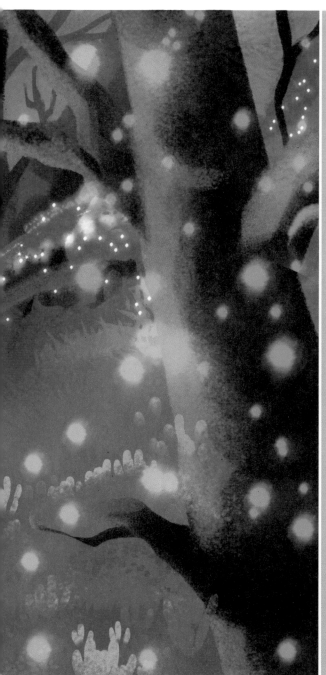

WHAT'S IN A NAME?

The name hippopotamus comes from the Greek language. "Hippo" means "horse," and "potamus" means "river." The name takes into account both a hippo's physical appearance and their habitat. This is a particularly apt description for pygmy hippos, who spend much of their time resting in rivers or swamps. They are believed to be messengers for water spirits and are linked to rainfall and prosperity.

PYGMY FRIENDS

PYGMY OWL

Unlike most other owls, which are nocturnal, pygmy owls hunt during the day. They sit very still before surprising their prey.

BORNEO PYGMY ELEPHANT

These elephants are found in the rainforests of Borneo, an island in Southeast Asia. Unlike pygmy hippos, pygmy elephants are sociable and live in groups of around eight, led by a female.

TAMARAW

Tamaraws are a dwarf buffalo found on the island of Mindoro in the Philippines. There are only around 300 individuals remaining.

Pygmy hippos aren't the only animals that are much smaller than their relatives. But being small has big benefits! Pygmy animals can move more easily through tricky terrain, and their tiny size makes them less easy for predators to spot.

PYGMY JERBOA

Despite being only around 2 in (5 cm) in length, pygmy jerboas can jump almost 9 ft (2.7 m) into the air!

PYGMY SEAHORSE

Pygmy seahorses can change color to blend in with the coral they live on. Because they're so hard to see—they're less than 1 in (2.5 cm) long—scientists aren't sure how many species of pygmy seahorse there are!

GLOSSARY

Amphibians
A type of animal that typically spends some of its life in water and some on land, such as frogs.

Bite force
The strength of an animal's jaw when it bites down.

Breeding
When animals mate to produce babies.

Climate change
A change in Earth's climate over time that can be natural or caused by human activity. This is making the planet hotter and weather more extreme.

Conservation
The protection of wildlife species, their habitats, and ecosystems.

Deforestation
The removal of a forest so the land can be used for other purposes.

Ecosystem
Living things and their environment and how they all interact with each other.

Endangered
A species with very low population numbers that is at risk of going extinct.

Extinct
When a species dies out and no longer exists.

Fragmented
When an area of land, such as a forest, is broken up so different parts of it are no longer connected.

Metabolism
The way the body converts the food and drink it consumes into energy to help it function properly.

Nocturnal
Describes animals that are most active at night.

Poaching
The illegal hunting of wildlife.

Predator
An animal that kills and eats other animals.

Prey
An animal that is killed and eaten by other animals.

Swamp
An area of low-lying land that is partially covered in water some of the time.

Traditional medicine
Treatments that are based on cultural or historical beliefs.

Undergrowth
Plants and shrubs that grow low down on the forest floor.

Wallowing
When large animals lie in water or mud to keep cool.

INDEX

This has been a

NEON 🦑 SQUID
production

To my wonderful niece and nephew Jessica and Edward—may this book remind you to always be curious about the world around you. I hope this story gives all readers a love of the natural world and inspires the next generation of conservationists.

Author: Dr. Fiona Sach
Illustrator: Lisa Maria

Design: Collaborate Agency
Senior Editor: Vicky Armstrong
US Editor: Jill Freshney
Proofreader: Joseph Barnes

Copyright © 2025
St. Martin's Press
120 Broadway, New York,
NY 10271

Created for St. Martin's Press
by Neon Squid
The Smithson, 6 Briset Street,
London, EC1M 5NR

EU representative: Macmillan
Publishers Ireland Ltd,
1st Floor, The Liffey Trust Centre,
117–126 Sheriff Street Upper,
Dublin 1, D01 YC43

10 9 8 7 6 5 4 3 2 1

The right of Dr. Fiona Sach to be
identified as the author of this
work has been asserted in
accordance with the Copyright,
Designs and Patents Act 1988.

All rights reserved. No part
of this publication may be
reproduced, stored in a retrieval
system, or transmitted, in
any form or by any means
(electronic, mechanical,
photocopying, recording or
otherwise), without the prior
written permission of
the publisher.

Library of Congress
Cataloging-in-Publication
Data is available.

Printed and bound in Maryland,
USA by Phoenix Color.

ISBN: 978-1-684-49589-4

Published in April 2025.

www.neonsquidbooks.com

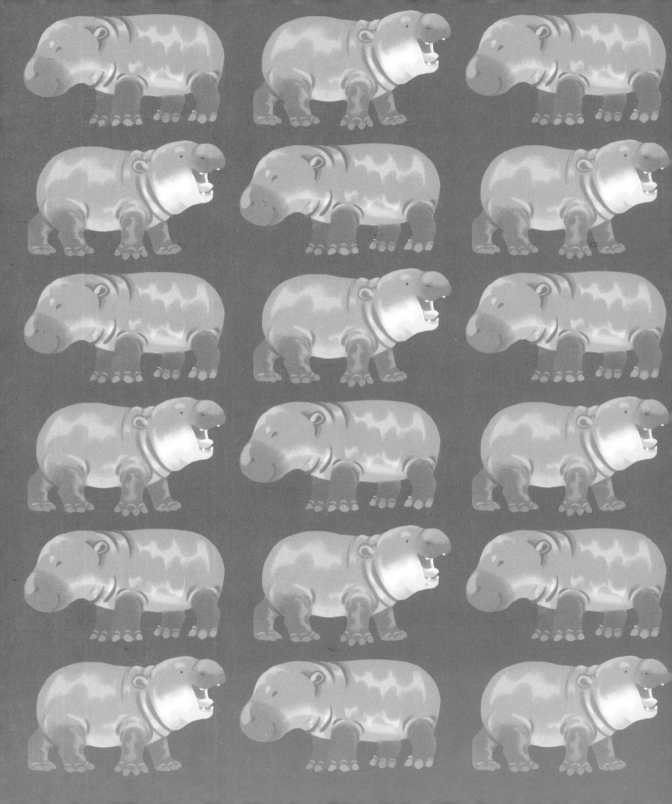